INCREDIBLY DISGUSTING DRUGS

ECSTASY AND YOUR HEART
The Incredibly Disgusting Story

Scott P. Werther

the rosen publishing group's
rosen central
new york

This book is for my parents and grandparents.

Published in 2001 by The Rosen Publishing Group, Inc.
29 East 21st Street, New York, NY 10010

Library of Congress Cataloging-in-Publication Data

Werther, Scott P.
Ecstasy and your heart / by Scott P. Werther.— 1st ed.
p. cm. — (Incredibly disgusting drugs)
Includes bibliographical references and index.
ISBN 0-8239-3390-3 (alk. paper)
1. Ecstasy (Drug)—Juvenile literature. 2. Heart—Effect of drugs on—Juvenile literature. [1. Ecstasy (Drug) 2. Drug abuse.]
I. Title. II. Series.
RM666.M35 W475 2000
615'.7883—dc21

00-011393

Manufactured in the United States of America

CONTENTS

Introduction

The word "ecstasy" makes us think of pleasant images. If we tried to create a mental picture of what ecstasy means, we might think of a movie scene where a young couple in love runs across a field of grass while holding hands. Another image could be that of a young child getting exactly what he or she wants for his or her birthday. Ecstasy is also the street name given to the drug MDMA (methylenedioxymethamphetamine).

Ecstasy is being widely abused by younger and younger kids—even twelve- or thirteen-year-olds. During the '90s in Dallas and New York, the drug gained popularity as the fuel for illegal all-night dance parties. These parties are known as raves, and they are often held in abandoned warehouses and other out-of-the-way places.

The spread of ecstasy was fueled by the growing popularity of raves in urban nightlife during the 1990s.

However, the drug has long since left its underground status behind, meaning that more and more people—often kids your age—are taking ecstasy. And the health risks of the drug are growing, too. One of the reasons for this is because the drug manufacturers are mainly interested in making a profit. These are not the type of people who are going to win the Nobel Peace Prize for their kindness toward humankind.

What a pill sold as ecstasy actually contains is anyone's guess. In the interest of saving money, ecstacy is "being cut," a street-slang term meaning that the pills are being manufactured with a number of cheaper drugs added in. The new additives include over-the-counter medicines, as well as the ingredients commonly found in cough syrup. DXM, or dextromethorphan, a common ingredient in cough syrup, speeds up the heart, raises blood pressure, and inhibits sweating. Many dealers claim that what they are giving you is pure ecstasy, but the reality is that they are more interested in your twenty to thirty dollars per pill than they are concerned about what their product will do to you. Dealers do not manufacture the drug and therefore do not really know what it contains. MDMA, which is the primary ingredient in "pure" ecstasy, has a negative effect on the brain and heart, but the cheaper drugs found in today's ecstasy are even more harmful to the body.

ECSTASY AND THE PURSUIT OF HAPPINESS

Even the healthiest people don't feel happy all of the time. A drug-induced high can alter emotions and moods for a brief period of time, making an unhappy person feel good again. Drugs are often abused by people who want to fill a void in their lives. Tragic events, difficult bouts of depression, and even everyday loneliness can cause a person to seek refuge in the temporary pleasures of drug use. Some people think that they can artificially control their emotional well-being.

Unfortunately, drug use doesn't solve the difficulties in our lives. In fact, it often makes them much worse. The little pill known as ecstasy earns its name because it makes the user feel good for a brief period of time. The MDMA in the pill is responsible for the euphoric high that users experience. The price for this euphoria is paid when the user crashes and experiences an intense down period. Ecstasy may jump-start the brain into feeling its finest for a few hours, but as we will learn in the following chapters, it may wind up taking a week or more for the brain to recover its normal functions.

What to Look Forward to—Brain Damage and Depression

Ecstasy users generally regard their drug of choice as being safer than heroin and cocaine. They argue that it is not as addictive or harmful to their health as other drugs, and they also claim that it has a therapeutic effect. This is a brilliant way to downplay the pursuit of manufactured, rather than real, happiness. Some words used to describe an ecstasy high are "peaceful," "empathetic," and "ener-getic." The positive effects start about half an hour after taking the drug and generally last for a few hours. The negative effects, however, linger much longer. Ecstasy acts on the receptors (the part of the neuron where neurotrans-mitters are absorbed) and may permanently damage the brain's ability to absorb serotonin. Serotonin is a neuro-transmitter in the brain that allows a person to feel pleas-ant sensations. A lack of serotonin can lead to depression. Even a single use of ecstasy impacts the serotonin to such an extent that it takes at least a week or two to recover the brain's normal ability to experience pleasure. This process will be explained in a later chapter.

Ecstasy—Just Like "Mystery Meat"

In the coming chapters, we will look at the functioning of the brain and heart, and we will also explore the impact that ecstasy has on these organs. In order to understand the risks associated with taking a pill containing questionable ingredients, think of the "mystery meat"—with its delicate green and brown hue—that you were served in elementary school and that was scooped, rather than placed, onto your tray. The reason for these distinctive colors was that the

The ingredients in ecstasy can be as random as the contents of "mystery meat."

ingredients for this "meat product" could have come from a wide variety of places, such as the slaughterhouse floor, or from the rodents that may have happened to run along the bins where the meat was being processed. What was actually sliding down your throat along with the salt and grease was the "mystery." With ecstasy, swallowing a "mystery" pill won't merely make your intestines revolt. The unknown ingredients can have an immediate and lasting effect on the most important organs in your body.

1 Ecstasy: How, What, Where, and Why

Since the mid-1990s, the abuse of ecstasy has begun to get out of hand to the extent that the government is raising penalties for dealers so that they are as harsh as those received by people who sell heroin or crack. The drug itself has been around for quite a while.

THE HISTORY BEHIND ECSTASY

MDMA was first patented in 1914 to E. Merck, a German company that was developing a diet drug. However, the drug was never tested on humans and was shelved for forty years. In 1953, the U.S. Army funded a study that explored the effects of a number of drugs that

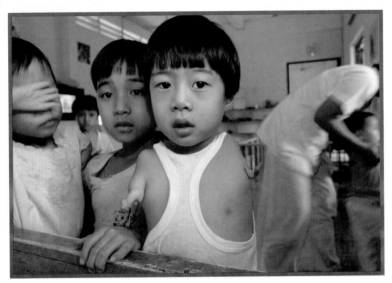

The U.S. Army shelved plans to use MDMA as a chemical weapon—the drug would have been effective only in large doses and could cause birth defects.

could potentially be used in chemical warfare. MDMA was tested, but it was not found to be harmful enough to kill people, except in dangerously large doses. A drug that was investigated by the U.S. Army for its potential to kill people is not the best choice for mental and physical health.

The Answer to Problem Marriages?

The drug resurfaced in the 1980s, when a few psycho-therapists began using it in therapy sessions with couples who were experiencing marriage problems. The drug produced a temporary sense of empathy between people that helped them open up to each other and work out their problems. However, this practice did not continue for long because the drug experience was not easily controlled. The odds were just as likely that the drug would create further problems between a husband and wife because of the drug's tendency to create anxiety and panic in the user. While taking ecstasy recreationally, one woman experienced such intense memories of a childhood trauma that it resulted in a depression that stayed with her for a few months. MDMA also made a brief appearance at some clubs where it was sold to patrons along with their drinks. Concerns about the effect that MDMA may have on the brain led the Drug Enforcement Agency (DEA) to declare it a Schedule I drug, which means that it has no clinical value.

HOW IT MAKES YOU FEEL

Ecstasy comes in many forms: a powder that is snorted, a pill (the most common form) that is swallowed, and a liquid that is injected into a vein. A half hour to an hour after an ecstasy pill is taken, the drug begins to take effect, though with snorting or injecting (which is much less common), a high is induced within five or ten minutes. The user will begin to feel a rush of energy and a sense of alertness. Ecstasy users also experience a peaceful empathy, which means that users act friendly to everyone around them, even if those people happen to be strangers. The drug also makes people very talkative, so that users may end up having long conversations about absolutely nothing on absolutely any subject—the spots on the floor, for instance. This effect peaks in the first hour or two and fades out altogether within four to six hours. The actual duration and intensity of an ecstasy high is influenced by a number of factors, such as environment, body type, and the purity of the pill. Afterward, the body needs a recovery period that typically lasts for at least a few days and, occasionally, even a week or two.

MESSING WITH YOUR MIND— PRETTY SCARY STUFF

There are many other negative effects that the drug may immediately inflict on a user. Ecstasy often causes such intense anxiety that a user feels the need to constantly clench his or her teeth. Becoming way too talkative—a side effect that seems harmless at first—can easily backfire. Many users have complained that they have revealed too much personal information while on ecstasy or have said something foolish that they later came to regret. And as

13

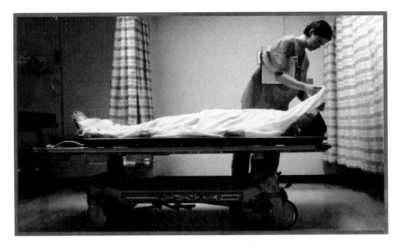

Ecstasy can cause users to overheat, sometimes with deadly results.

we all know, telling a stranger where you live or what your phone number is can lead to grave consequences.

In addition, sometimes a user's reaction to the drug can be so intense that a panic attack or a bout of extreme paranoia will ensue. And as with all drugs, when a person takes ecstasy, his or her usual sense of inhibition will no longer be in effect—a situation that can often lead to poor choices. This can be extremely dangerous if the user is not in an entirely safe environment. Any situation where drugs are being used, even a protected, controlled environment, carries this risk because drugs are capable of bringing out the worst in otherwise trustworthy people.

The risk of personal injury while on drugs is as great as the health risks of the drug itself. Ecstasy can also inhibit sweating, which is actually the body's ability to cool itself. If this occurs, the user can become overheated. In severe cases of overheating, people can die. This is perhaps the most dangerous short-term effect. Ecstasy-related deaths are frequently a result of the body overheating.

THE LURE OF ECSTASY—WHY PEOPLE WANT TO TAKE IT

The reasons people take ecstasy vary greatly. There is no single answer that can explain why a person decides to use drugs. Many people convince themselves that drugs can help them get through hard times, like a recent breakup of a relationship or the death of a loved one. Some people decide to use ecstasy because it is associated with a particular lifestyle that they want to take part of or imitate. Others use ecstasy as an attempt to feel like they belong to a certain group of people—in most cases, ravers. Ravers, ranging in age from fourteen to thirty-five, used to come from all walks of life. However, raves today are mostly attended by middle-class urban kids. Ecstasy is also used by people who are bored and who choose to seek out an artificial means of entertaining themselves.

Drugs Are Not the Answer

The high from ecstasy and other drugs may appear to be a quick release from life's problems. But in reality, these drugs often increase the difficulties in our lives by allowing us to forget about our problems instead of dealing with them. The drug itself usually causes a lot more problems—both mentally and physically—than were there to begin with. The more you abuse a particular drug, the more it becomes obvious that happiness can't be manufactured.

RAVES AND RAVERS

Even though ecstasy use is prevalent in many different social settings, this has not always been the case. Ecstasy started out as an underground drug that was primarily used at raves. These often-illegal, all-night dance parties have brought in more than 10,000 people. One recent Halloween rave in Toronto drew a crowd of 16,000. Raves have become increasingly popular since the early

'90s and are now a mainstream activity for many young people. It is at these raves that ecstasy use has evolved into a subculture with its own kind of clothes and music.

At a rave, some people take ecstasy so that they can dance all night to whatever form of electronic music happens to be playing, whether it be trance, industrial, or techno. Some people claim that ecstasy makes them feel very friendly, even toward strangers, which, as we know, is not always a good thing. It is easy to take advantage of someone who is on drugs. Many ravers choose to use drugs in an attempt to create an artificial and temporary sense of community.

Raves are not necessarily drug havens. In fact, many of them are even drug free. Their commercialization has led to a greater police presence, which means less illegal activity. Many teens have found raves to be an excellent outlet for parts of their personality that they have not been able to express in other ways.

Peace, Love, Unity, and Respect

These underground parties have even developed their own guiding principles that express a genuine concern for humanity—P.L.U.R. (peace, love, unity, and respect).

Raves were created to be a comfortable environment for all types of young people, a place where they could have fun without fear of ridicule. Ravers have even been called neohippies, a term that refers to the hippies of the 1960s, who also embraced peace and love.

Ecstasy use has shed a negative light on raves. Many people go to raves because they've heard that these dance parties are a place where drugs are sold and used, a rumor that has ended up ruining the spirit of dance parties. The crowd has shifted from accepting, open-minded people to those who are looking for a place to get an artificial high. This shift of focus from P.L.U.R. to drug use has caused many raves to be broken up by the police, and some participants have been arrested.

Raves that are about the music are still taking place, but, unfortunately, they are on the decline because of club drugs like ecstasy. Some past participants of raves don't go anymore because they no longer feel comfortable there. They claim that the focus of today's raves is on drug use and that it has ruined the once-friendly atmosphere. There are a significant number of ravers who still attend, though, but they choose to stay drug free because they feel it is a lot more fun that way.

THE LIFE CYCLE OF AN ECSTASY PILL

Ecstasy has a long life cycle even before it reaches the hands of youth. It is manufactured in underground labs found mostly in rural areas in European countries such as the Netherlands and Poland. The raw ingredients are stored in large barrels described by one law enforcement official as being "so filthy, I wouldn't even keep my garbage in it."

Today's ecstasy is made from a wide variety of chemicals, some of which have been proven to have fatal results when ingested. These chemicals are combined in underground labs typically run by an organized crime ring. The way the pills are distributed and smuggled into the United States occurs in a number of different ways. It is tricky for drug smugglers to get the ecstasy from the place of manufacture to countries where the pills will yield the biggest profit. Because of this, smugglers have developed elaborate schemes, with the most common mode of transport being commercial airlines flying into highly trafficked areas such as JFK and Newark Airports in the New York City area. This is one of the biggest markets for ecstasy. Since the drug has only recently seen a rise in popularity, police have just

Beware of this dog—he is trained to detect illegal drugs.

begun to train dogs to sniff out MDMA and post them at many airports. Because of this tight security, criminals have to be much smarter and more creative. Once the ecstasy has made it into the United States, it is distributed by drug lords who purchase ecstasy in large amounts and then sell it to individual dealers. It is these dealers who sell the drugs in schools, on the streets, and in clubs.

The Price Is Right

Even though ecstasy is fairly expensive to purchase, it is very cheap to make, costing about ten cents a pill. Because

Under today's strong drug laws, possession of ecstasy could land you in prison for a long time.

of the high profit margin, a number of drug lords who formerly made their money off of heroin and cocaine have turned to ecstasy instead. These drug lords operate in highly organized crime rings, some of which are run by members of the Mafia. Sammy "the Bull" Gravano was a mob hitman turned drug lord who got arrested recently for selling large amounts of ecstasy to high school and college students. He used gangs of teenagers known for their violent acts to distribute the drug. He also involved many members of his family—who are now behind bars with him—in his drug ring.

Trying to Stop the Trafficking of Ecstasy

As a response to the rising abuse of ecstasy, laws have been passed that make sure that dealers and users suffer much harsher consequences. Great efforts are being made to stop the spread of the drug. There is increased security in airports and more pressure on foreign governments to crack down on drug distribution. The fines and jail time for the possession and distribution of ecstasy have more than tripled. Getting involved with ecstasy is certainly not as safe as some users claim when attempting to convince their friends to give the drug a try.

THE DANGERS OF HERBAL ECSTASY

In the early '90s, some drug manufacturers noticed the ecstasy trend and developed their own legal imitation drug. The drug these people marketed, ephedrine, is actually a natural stimulant. It does not affect the user in the same way as MDMA. Herbal ecstasy affects the body by raising blood pressure and by making the skin tingle and the heart race. Promoting and selling ephedrine as an alternative to ecstasy is clever and deceptive.

You might think heart attacks happen only to older adults, but if you take herbal ecstasy, it could happen to you.

Herbal ecstasy is often sold under the false pretense of being natural, but it certainly is not healthy or even safe. It is typically taken in large doses in an attempt to mirror the effects of MDMA. It produces many of the same negative side effects experienced by ecstasy users. When taken in large doses, herbal ecstasy has also been linked to heart attacks, seizures, and death. Some states have stopped selling ephedrine, and the Food and Drug Administration (FDA) has issued a health warning against it. What herbal ecstasy and ecstasy sold on the street have most in common is that they are both drugs capable of harming the body.

2 Your Heart

Most people don't realize that the human heart is really a big muscle. Exercise strengthens the heart just like it does the muscles in our legs and arms. Ecstasy takes a great toll on the body—especially the heart. Let's look at what happens when the heart beats so that we can better understand the ill effects that ecstasy and other drugs have on the functioning of this vital organ.

HOW THE HEART WORKS

The heart is so important that if it stops for even a few minutes, you can die. Over the course of our lives, our hearts never stop working. The human heart beats about two and a half billion times in an average lifetime. The heart has been referred to as a "pumping machine" because it works—without rest—at circulating blood to all parts of the body. When we sleep, the heart slows down, and when we go running or do other strenuous activities, it speeds up. In an average healthy person, the cardiac muscles of the heart beat about seventy to eighty times a minute, meaning that the adult heart pumps about 4,300 gallons of blood in a single day!

The heart has four main parts, called chambers, through which blood is pumped. These chambers are separated from one another by valves. The valves are open when blood flows the correct way through the heart. The valves close to prevent the blood from going backward through the heart. When the heart expands, it pulls blood into the right atrium in the heart. When it contracts, the blood is forced out of the right atrium and into the right ventricle. The heart's contraction then squeezes the blood into the pulmonary artery where it is carried into the lungs. Nerves connected to the heart regulate the speed of the contractions.

To gain a better understanding of how a beating heart works, think of your middle school science class. You probably used an eyedropper for many different experiments. If you squeezed the rubber part of the dropper and stuck the other end in a sink of water, what would happen? Water would be sucked up into the dropper. This is similar to the expansion of the heart when blood is brought into the right atrium. Squeeze it again and the water is forced out. This is similar to the contraction of the heart when blood is moved into the right ventricle and the pulmonary artery. Your hand acts as the nerves that control the speed of the contractions.

If you think this seems like a lot of work, you're correct. It's no secret that the heart is a delicate organ that is essential to our survival. What is surprising is that so many people are willing to risk damaging it for a temporary high. Though the heart is a strong muscle, it is also extremely vulnerable to the foreign substances that we put in our bodies. In an adult human, the heart is only about as big as a fist and weighs an average of eleven ounces. As a middle schooler, your heart probably weighs eight or nine ounces. That's not very big for such an important organ.

Ecstasy's Journey to the Heart—Risky Business

Ecstasy comes in many forms, including a powder that is snorted, a pill that is swallowed, and a liquid that is injected into a vein. All of these methods of drug abuse

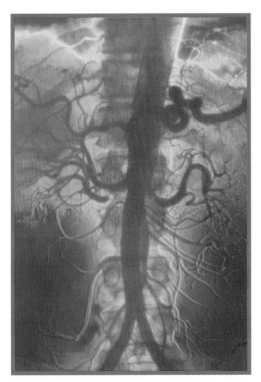

When ingested, MDMA rushes through the bloodstream and disturbs the heart's natural rhythm.

place MDMA in your bloodstream, where it is whisked away directly to the heart. When it enters the heart, the natural pumping process is disturbed. Ecstasy causes the heart to beat much faster than normal. The speeding up of the heart can be healthy when someone is running because it increases strength. Disturbing the heart's natural rhythm with ecstasy is very dangerous because MDMA damages the cardiac muscles. MDMA also increases blood pressure.

Is It Really Worth It?

Some people are born with heart defects that may go unnoticed. These defects may never affect or shorten

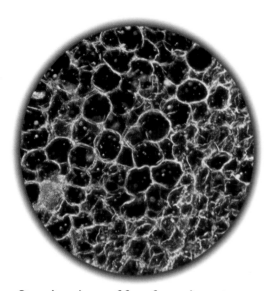

People who suffer from heart conditions are especially prone to the adverse effects of ecstasy.

their lives. However, even a single dose of ecstasy can kill a person with a heart condition. Does ecstasy use really seem worth the risk of death or serious injury? Is it that important to feel friendlier toward strangers for a short period of time?

The combination of high blood pressure and increased heart rate that result from ecstasy use has also proven to be fatal for a number of otherwise healthy people. Physical activity quickens a heart rate that is already unnaturally fast. And since a lot of ecstasy is taken at raves or at other social events where the user is already active, ecstasy use becomes an even greater risk. Since today's ecstasy also contains so many substances other than MDMA, there's no way to know what else is in the pill and what effect these mystery ingredients could have on someone's already overworked heart.

3 Your Brain

Ecstasy also has a significant impact on the brain. In order to understand the effects the drug has on its users, we need to look at how the brain processes pleasure. Think of one of those science museum exhibits where a ball rolls through an elaborate course that sets in motion a chain of events.

The ball drops onto a track and rolls through a series of loops before falling onto a wheel that lights a bulb when it spins. This sequence of events is similar to the chemical process that occurs in a person's brain when he or she feels pleasure. Just as the ball dropping onto the track eventually leads to the bulb being lit, the electrical impulse originating in the brain leads to the release of serotonin. The brain's equivalent to the metal track that the ball rolls on is the nerve cell, or neuron. Serotonin is a common chemical in the brain that acts as a neurotransmitter, which means that it is responsible for relaying signals to different parts of the brain. Just as the ball rolls down the track, the electrical impulse travels down the axon. Instead of a bulb being lit, an electrical pulse is sent down the next neuron.

SEROTONIN AND FEELING GOOD

Serotonin—a neurotransmitter that transmits messages from neuron to neuron—has a profound effect on our moods. Serotonin also has a direct influence on our sex drive, appetite, and sleep. When we feel good, our brain is being flooded with serotonin. When you score the winning goal and feel great when everyone swarms the field to hug you, serotonin is being released in your brain. When you fall in love with someone and feel mushy when he or she is around, your serotonin is kicking in. Even just listening to good music and driving around with your friends can cause serotonin to be released in your brain.

In order to understand the effects that serotonin has on the brain, you need to look at a part of the brain referred to as "the cellar"—the raphne nucleus. From

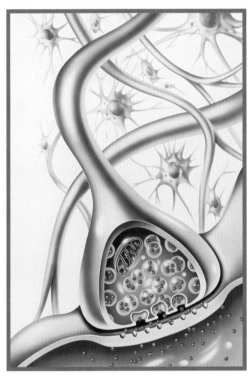

Ecstasy can seriously affect the levels of the neurotransmitter serotonin in the human brain.

here, serotonin neurons reach to other places in the brain with vinelike extensions called axons. These axons can be up to a foot long, though they are far too thin to be seen with the naked eye. The raphne nucleus sends an electrical pulse into the first part of a neuron, called the dendrite, and then up the axon. At the end of the axon is the axon terminal, which resembles coral and is used to send messages to the next neuron.

Serotonin is stored in the axon terminal in vesicles. When the electrical signal reaches the terminal, the serotonin is released from these vesicles. These neurons connect various regions of the brain.

The axon terminal is the end of a neuron. The beginning of the next neuron is the dendrite. Even though these neurons are responsible for relaying messages, they never touch. The space between them is the synapse. On the edge of the dendrite are receptors that absorb some of the serotonin released into the synapse by the axon terminal. The amount of serotonin released into the synapse has been shown to have a direct effect on our moods. The more that is released, the happier we feel. After the serotonin is absorbed by the receptors, another electrical impulse travels down the next neuron. This chain-reaction effect is how neurons transmit messages to other parts of the brain.

The reuptake of serotonin is an essential step in the chemical reactions of pleasure processing. It is how the brain is able to regulate emotions. Not all of the serotonin floating around in the synapse is absorbed by the dendrite. Some is taken back into the axon terminal. This process is referred to as reuptake. It ensures that we always have a consistent amount of serotonin in our brains. This consistency affords us an emotional balance because a ready supply of serotonin means that we always have the capability of feeling pleasure.

ECSTASY'S EFFECT ON THE BRAIN

Once it is taken, ecstasy goes right into the brain and tricks it into releasing the chemicals that make us feel pleasure. It short-circuits the brain by directly interfering with the process of serotonin release and reuptake by causing the vesicles to release serotonin from the axon terminal. The MDMA causes most of the serotonin to be released. This floods the synapse with an unusually high amount of the neurotransmitter and is responsible for the euphoric high experienced by an ecstasy user. In fact, so much of the brain's serotonin is used that the high is maintained for two or three hours. This high is also a result of the MDMA having an effect on the reuptake process in the brain. The MDMA prevents the serotonin that has been released into the synapse from being absorbed back into the axon terminal. This means that all of the serotonin will eventually be absorbed by the dendrite. This process takes a few hours and is responsible for a temporary high.

Like Ecstasy? Then Say Good-Bye to Feeling Good

The high from ecstasy is very temporary and ultimately hurts the user more than it helps. Since MDMA blocks the reuptake process, the brain cannot maintain its natural reserve supply of serotonin. MDMA causes so much serotonin to be released that it can take about two weeks for the brain to replenish its supply and accumulate more normal levels. This

Ecstasy use can cause extended bouts of deep depression.

lack of serotonin causes the ecstasy user to feel depressed when he or she crashes (when the effects of the drug have worn off). Hence, the ecstasy user pays a price for the chance of a few hours of pleasure. Many who use ecstasy learn the hard way that nothing is worth feeling down for weeks on end.

It's Really Not Worth It

Since ecstasy abuse is a more recent phenomenon than heroin or cocaine abuse, there is a lot more to be learned about how it affects the brain. There have been a few studies, and the information that they have released is alarming. MDMA has been shown to cause long-term and even permanent damage in the brains of animals. One study found that even a single use of the drug had the potential to hurt the brain for

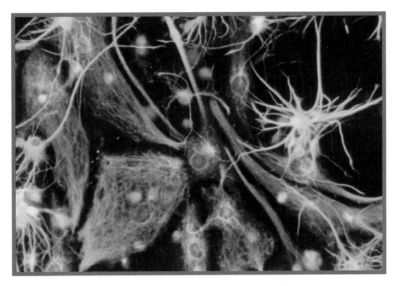

This is a picture of healthy nerve cells. There have been studies that show that using ecstasy can irreversibly damage human nerve cells.

much longer than a few weeks. It has been reported that ecstasy can damage nerve cells to such an extent that they never grow back. This prevents the neurons from transmitting the electrical impulses that communicate pleasure to all parts of the brain. Although these studies are too recent to be considered conclusive, they've definitely proven that taking ecstasy is a risky gamble.

4 Coping with an Ecstasy Problem

Ed was an intelligent and open-minded guy. He spent a lot of time in class staring out the window or drawing characters on his notebooks. Ed spent a lot of time alone. It was hard for him to be talkative around people he didn't know very well, so he avoided them. He knew a lot of the popular kids in school, but he never wanted to hang out with them. Ed was generally bored by school life and never knew what to do in his free time. He agreed to go to the rave when his friend Matt called because there was nothing better going on.

When they arrived, Matt immediately found a group of girls he knew and went off to dance with them. Ed had been hanging around the outside of the dance floor for a while when Mike approached him and said, "You look like

Using ecstasy, in addition to causing depression and anxiety, can also suppress one's appetite.

you're not having any fun. Do you want to liven things up a bit?" "Why not?" Ed said to himself as he swallowed the little pill with a design stamped on it.

Before long, Ed really felt the desire to dance. He ended up staying at the rave all night. He had many long conversations with people, though he couldn't really remember them very well. During the next week he felt very depressed and didn't feel like eating. He also suffered from anxiety attacks. He went to another rave the next weekend and found Mike, who charged him thirty dollars

Depression and anxiety can change your normal
habits and make you distracted and lazy.

*for an ecstasy pill. Ed danced all night but didn't have as
much fun as before. That following week, his depression
reached an all-time low. Soon Ed could think only about
going to the rave, mainly so that he could feel better. Every
few nights, he sneaked out of his parents' house. He felt
more distracted at school, and instead of his usual reading,
Ed watched television every night because it passed the
time quicker.*

*One Tuesday night when Ed was at the rave, the kid
dancing next to him collapsed on the dance floor. His skin*

was pale and yellow and he had stopped breathing. At the end of the night, Ed had a pounding headache. The police came into the rave and arrested a number of people.

The next day at school, Ed found out that the kid who collapsed was Steve from his English class. The school called a special assembly and explained that Steve had died. He had swallowed ecstasy that was laced with a number of toxic chemicals. These chemicals had caused Steve's body to lose its natural ability to sweat. Steve had died from overheating because his body lost its ability to cool itself.

That night, Ed called Matt, even though he was worried about what he might think. Ed explained what he had been doing for the past few months. Matt listened calmly and, together, they figured out some strategies that Ed could use to beat his drug problem.

SIGNS OF ECSTASY ABUSE

Not everyone who uses ecstasy has an eye-opening experience like Ed did. More and more people are sharing the same fate as Steve. Ecstasy abuse is often not as obvious as that of its fellow Class A drugs—cocaine and heroin. Parties and raves are often the breeding grounds for frequent ecstasy use because they provide a comfortable environment for drug users. In recent years, many people have come to these parties just because they can use drugs there without fear of being looked down upon. Many young people find the rave world philosophy of P.L.U.R. to be a welcome relief from what they considered the coldheartedness of the rest of the world. It is unfortunate that some people in this same environment encourage and promote drug use. This has given an unnecessarily dangerous edge to raves and has killed many young people.

Ecstasy abusers, like many other drug users, often structure their lives around the next high. Ed's story is pretty common. For someone who has let his or her happiness depend on ecstasy, the rest of the world can become pretty grim. Many people lose sight of their previous interests, as Ed did, or don't take time to find new ones, because they make ecstasy their number one priority. Being addicted to a drug means surrendering your life to it. One of the first symptoms is that the user doesn't feel, or even care, that he or she has a problem. Ed didn't seem bothered that he spent all of his free time thinking about being in the club. Life without ecstasy can lead a user to become irritable and dissatisfied with his or her environment. It is important to be able to recognize the signs of a problem if you or someone you care about is abusing drugs. Perhaps you, or someone you know, has a problem like Ed's.

WHAT YOU CAN DO TO HELP

What can you do if you feel that someone you know has an ecstasy problem? First of all, don't scare yourself senseless. Even though chronic drug use may seem like a hopeless situation, many past users have been able to turn their lives around. Often, the hardest step is recognizing the signs of a problem.

Ed continued to sneak out more and more because he didn't see anything wrong with his drug use. It is easy for a person to deny that his or her drug use is a problem, or claim that it is a phase that will pass. Yet, if things have reached a point where someone else is starting to become concerned, it is probably the right time for a reality check. If the person with the problem is approached calmly, he or she may be more willing to understand that his or her drug use is a cause for concern. It is important that someone with a drug problem recognize that he or she isn't living up to his or her true potential. This allows the person to see the problem as his or her own and not blame it on others. It is also important to listen—as Matt did—and not judge someone for their drug abuse. Accept the fact that things usually don't change overnight. It is up to the person with the problem to recognize it. All anyone else can do is help him or her see it.

Many Ways of Getting Help

Humans have had drug problems for centuries before you were even born. Knowing this may provide little comfort, but what it means is that there have been a lot of methods developed to assist those with drug problems. It may not be easy to quit if you are the one with the problem, but it will be well worth it in the long run. Try out a variety of different methods. Talk to a discussion group or to a therapist. Remove yourself for a while from the environment that encouraged you to try drugs in the first place. More important, go out and try something healthy that you've never done before. If you like music, pick up an instrument. If you like to read, try writing. There are plenty of things to get excited about in life. It's up to you to figure out what will give you the natural high that drugs try to imitate.

GLOSSARY

axon   Vinelike extension that transmits electrical signals to different regions in the brain.

ephedrine   Natural stimulant that has similar effects to ecstasy.

MDMA   Drug that later came to be known as ecstasy.

neuron   A nerve cell in the brain.

neurotransmitter   Chemical that relays messages from one part of the brain to another.

pulmonary artery   Part of the circulatory system that takes blood to the lungs.

serotonin   Neurotransmitter in the brain that controls the sex drive, appetite, and sleep.

FOR MORE INFORMATION

In the United States

Narcotics Anonymous
World Service Office
P.O. Box 9999
Van Nuys, CA 91409
(818) 773-9999
Web site: http://www.na.org

National Clearinghouse for
Alcohol and Drug
Information
P.O. Box 2345
Rockville, MD 20847-2345
(800) 729-6686
Web site:
http://www.health.org

The National Institute on
Drug Abuse
National Institutes of
Health (NIH)
Bethesda, MD 20892-9651
6001 Executive Boulevard,
Room 5213
(301) 443-1124
Web site:
http://www.nida.nih.gov

Partnership for a Drug-
Free America
405 Lexington Avenue,
Suite 1601
New York, NY 10174
(212) 922-1560
Web site: http://www.
drugfreeamerica.org

In Canada

Canadian Centre on
Substance Abuse
75 Albert Street, Suite 300
Ottawa, ON K1P 5E7
(613) 235-4048
Web site: http://www.ccsa.ca

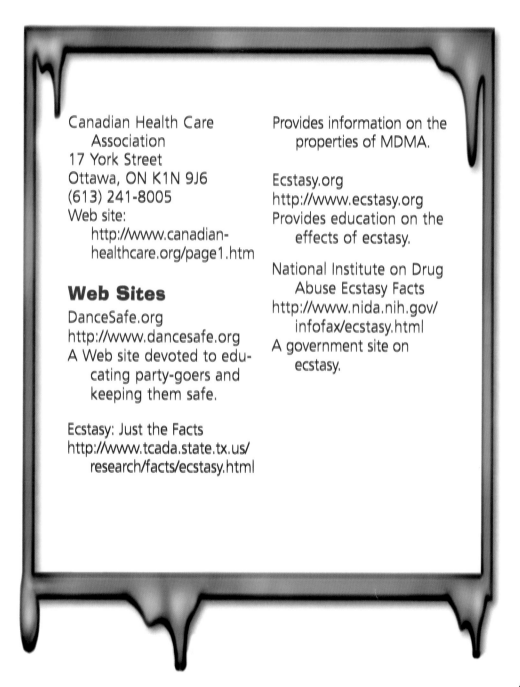

Canadian Health Care
    Association
17 York Street
Ottawa, ON K1N 9J6
(613) 241-8005
Web site:
    http://www.canadian-
    healthcare.org/page1.htm

Web Sites

DanceSafe.org
http://www.dancesafe.org
A Web site devoted to edu-
    cating party-goers and
    keeping them safe.

Ecstasy: Just the Facts
http://www.tcada.state.tx.us/
    research/facts/ecstasy.html

Provides information on the
    properties of MDMA.

Ecstasy.org
http://www.ecstasy.org
Provides education on the
    effects of ecstasy.

National Institute on Drug
    Abuse Ecstasy Facts
http://www.nida.nih.gov/
    infofax/ecstasy.html
A government site on
    ecstasy.

FOR FURTHER READING

Alvergue, Anne. *Ecstasy: The Danger of False Euphoria.* New York: The Rosen Publishing Group, Inc., 1998.

Brennan, Kristine. *Ecstasy and Other Designer Drugs.* Philadelphia: Chelsea House, 2000.

Cloud, John. "The Lure of Ecstasy." *Time*, June 5, 2000, pp. 62–73.

Cohen, Richard S. *The Love Drug: Marching to the Beat of Ecstasy.* New York: Haworth Press, 1998.

Glass, George. *Drugs and Fitting In.* New York: The Rosen Publishing Group, Inc., 1998.

Gutman, Bill. *Harmful to Your Health.* New York: Twenty-First Century Books, 1996.

Kuhn, Cynthia, Scott Swartzwelder, and Wilkie Wilson. *Buzzed: The Straight Facts About the Most Used and Abused Drugs from Alcohol to Ecstasy.* New York: W.W. Norton and Company, 1998.

Phillips, Lynn. *Drug Abuse.* New York: Marshall Cavendish, 1994.

Smith-McLaughlin, Miriam, and Sandra Peyser-Hazouri. *Addiction: The "High" That Brings You Down.* Springfield, NJ: Enslow Publishers, 1997.

INDEX

CREDITS

About the Author
Scott P. Werther lives in Queens, New York. He is a free-lance writer, and he recommends that you stay in school.

Photo Credits
Cover and p. 28 © Alfred Pasieka/Science Photo Library; cover insert © Tek image/Science Photo Library; p. 5 © Eric Mason Stringer/AP Wide World; p. 9 © Michael S. Yamashite/Corbis; p. 11 © Steve Raymer/Corbis; p. 14 © Franco Vogt/Corbis; p. 20 © Ralph A. Clevenger/Corbis; p. 21 © Earl Kogler - Corp. Media/International Stock Photo; p. 23 © Oskar Burriel/Latin Stock/SPL; p. 27 © CNRI/SPL; p. 31 © John Bavosi/SPL; pp. 34, 37, 38 Antonio Mari; p. 35 © Nancy Kedersha/UCLA/SPL.

Series Design
Laura Murawski